SUPER MODEL **MINORITY**

'*Super Model Minority* is tender and electric, full of quiet intimacy
and soaring elegy. In these shapeshifting poems, Tse confronts joy,
pain, prejudice, whiteness. His poems transform and shimmer
in full colour, calling back and forth to each other through the
book like a pop song's echoing refrain.'

— **Nina Mingya Powles**

'*Super Model Minority* is the brilliant and important new Chris Tse
collection that you need in your life right now, and forever. More
bold, more beautiful, more raw, more artful and more funny
than ever before – these poems cut my heart before warming it,
got me squirming awkwardly in my seat and made me determined
to visit Iceland before I die.'

— **Helen Rickerby**

'This collection by Chris Tse is like the glitter bomb that heralds
the apocalypse. It's a reminder that life is a prismatic experience
full of heartbreak, oh-so-predictable racism and awkward family
games nights. It asks us to stop and consider all the aspects of
ourselves that we want to take into the future, and how they are
shaped by the histories we leave behind.'

— **Rose Lu**

CHRIS TSE

SUPER MODEL MINORITY

AUCKLAND
UNIVERSITY
PRESS

First published 2022
Auckland University Press
University of Auckland
Private Bag 92019
Auckland 1142
New Zealand
www.aucklanduniversitypress.co.nz

ISBN 978 1 86940 961 6

Published with the assistance of Creative New Zealand

A catalogue record for this book is available from
the National Library of New Zealand

Design by Greg Simpson

This book was printed on FSC® certified paper

Printed in Singapore by Markono Print Media Pte Ltd

This book is for my parents.

Contents

Poetry to make boys cry

Study the past if you would define the future.

— Confucius

... tomorrows keep on blowing in from somewhere.

— Bic Runga

Utopia? BIG MOOD!

I will use my tongue for good.   I say *I will*
because this book needs to start with the future   even though the future
has always scared me   with its metallic fingernails poking through
the metaphysical portal   come-hithering.   Aspiration—and the threat
of what we have awakened from the salty ashes of a world gone mad—
aspiration will bolster my stretch goals.   I will   use my tongue to taste
utopia, and share its delights with my minority brothers and sisters
before the unmarked vans arrive to usher me back in time. Each set
of curtains I pass through is a sucker punch—a reason to doubt my own
optimism. I'm mostly careless in that regard.   The future scares me,
but it's good to be scared of what I want, even if it means that
the more I write, the more I grieve   for something I'm not even sure
belongs to me.   Perhaps I don't belong in utopia—perhaps
there isn't a place for me under its many suns and moons, so to be thrown
backwards every time we approach the future is history's way of
telling me I'm in a loop I should just lean into.   I want to know why
there isn't a place for me.   Perhaps it's because I ask too many questions
about who will change the direction of the river.   They say I make
a fuss of the past as they drag me through it again and again to put me
in my place.   Can you blame me
for attempting to reverse-engineer utopia as a means of survival?
All the good in the world is set to expire when its afflictions become
too much, when I am a length of string tied to a pole in an open field
cut loose from my other end—just left to twist in the wind
waiting for someone kind enough to tether me.   It doesn't matter
who, or to what.   It's all progress, I guess—even if there's no way
to measure it.   But I'll try—in the number of poems written, in keys
of songs, in gates torn down between here and wherever I think
I will belong, believing.   I said *I will*.

Super model minority

Wish list—Permadeath

I wish I didn't feel compelled to write about racism, but there it is
patrolling my everyday thoughts like a mall cop drunk with power.

I wish people didn't ask me how to solve a problem like racism, as if
it is a cloud they cannot pin down. I am not an expert spokesperson

holding an elusive truth. I wish I could predict when racism
would exit stage right to wherever bad things go to die rusty

non-biodegradable deaths, but I can't predict the death of something
with a robust business continuity plan that involves moving from

host body to host body. I am not an exorcist—I am a sympathetic
vomiter. Is it predictable for me to write this poem? I suppose so.

What I really want to write about are things with promise, to offer up
whiskers on kittens when the outlook is for Nazis upon Nazis. I wish

I could sing my way out of this while the man I love applauds from
the front row, our adorable Jack Russell terrier Rocket sat by his feet.

I wish I could start a love poem with a line like 'He thumbs me
like the *Oxford Dictionary*' and consider it a job well done. I wish

I didn't always feel this way—always tired of explaining why
I am tired and why writing this poem is more need than want.

I never felt the need to be the gunshot during a knife fight until they
told me there was no such thing as 'let's finish this once and for all'.

'I wish the racism were not so predictable.' — Chen Chen

I realise now nothing is ever truly finished. I get knocked out but I am
a flashing corpse regenerating in a video game with limited credits.

I guess there's always the pull of more to do—flags to fly and
words to scratch into the world's longest stretch of wet concrete.

I guess what I'm saying is—I am not done with snakes and wolves;
I am not done with feathers or glitter on the roof of my mouth.

This is me begging for a fountain to take all my wishes.
This is me speaking a storm into my every day.

Version control

It has come to my attention that we have fucked things up.
Not that we inherited the best bones to work with—some broken
a few too many times, others carelessly tossed into suitcases
that no one will ever claim. The bones don't always form a whole.

It's 1616 and they're publicly burning us to ashes for sodomy.
It's 1885 and they've made us criminals to protect decency.
It's 1998 and they're beating us, torturing us and tying us to fences.
It's 2021 and they're rediscovering old ways to erase us.

Each time we say it gets better, or that we will learn from the past,
we set ourselves up for crushing failure—jinxed and cursed,
a self-addressed envelope for a future that will never come
to pass. This time is no different from the all the last times.

In one version we were golden—our nights sweetly perfumed
by the sea breezes of childhood holidays and apple crumble
just out of the oven. We fail to mention that one year a young boy's
body washed ashore in non-accidental circumstances and, later,
bad wiring in the oven was the cause of our house burning down.

In another version, our days are drowned in blue screen light
electrifying our brains and keeping us up at night so that we
stew in the unmistakable stench of bodies rotting under the
floorboards. We buried our dead but we didn't bury the causes
of their deaths—and therein lies the seed of our predicament.

All these versions of the past are the same explosion replayed
at different speeds and our failure to act is the debris blacking out

the sun. We can't bury the lines between then-now and now-then
hoping no one will notice they're missing and go looking for them
to prove we haven't changed at all. We can't be that fucking naïve.

Tell me which version of the world you want to live in: the one
in which the definition of a body is a loaded gun waiting to be shot,
or the one in which the definition of hope is a meteorite passing
over our heads and disappearing into the uncharted skies?
Both are valid, but only one will let you sleep at night.

Karaoke for the end of the world

Racists and homophobes don't ask about the weather while they abuse you from moving cars, and although I wish to lead by example, killing them with kindness can only get us so far. There's a temptation to chase each car and ask, *How's your mother—how's your job—have you read any good tweets lately?* Small talk won't make a difference to the gleam of the guillotine blade that believes it has no choice but to fall edge first into every soft neck. In these moments I think *show backbone* but I forget the words and my ultimate flinch is to bury myself where they can't find me. Why am I embarrassed about my anger while others wield theirs so freely? But even with my tongue torn from my mouth I can still sing the saddest song, the most furious song—you too can follow along with the words as they glow radioactive. It goes a little something like … the earth yawning and unhinging its jaw or the sky relinquishing its guardian status, leaving you naked on the stage with only a microphone stand to hide behind. We would all benefit from a surprise key change in the middle of every traumatic experience. Dystopia cannot name the alternative in the same way a dog without its bark can improvise a warning to protect its master. This is a small thing that means everything. There might be a lesson in being called a chink or a fag in broad daylight—it has something to do with what's familiar that has gone missing. But it's the punchline in the disconnect that sticks with you, like performing a song about dancing with your father set to a montage of dung beetles rolling balls of shit, or a song about bling and popping champagne while doomed lovers stroll through the rain without an umbrella in scenes from a Korean soap opera. I have reduced myself to playing the part of empty orchestra far too many times to know what sort of reception I'll receive. I brace myself for hard hands on my slack body while the crowd films every grope on their phones. But this time I tip my head back and release the most primal sound I can summon, a reach so pained it can be understood by all creatures: a confession with no sigh of relief, a demand for consequences. I look them all in the eyes and the lyrics flicker in front of me: *Help   me.   I'm   dying   here.*

Super model minority — Flashbacks

I close my eyes and imagine what it might have felt like to make my way towards water in the darkness before fire. I'd listen out for giveaway sounds of motion among the chatter of birds, perhaps hesitate when forest floor turned to sand beneath my feet. I have no reason to doubt the breadth of all that is both knowable and unknown when anything could stain my mind. With eyes shut and fists clenched tight, I prepare for my body to be taken by what I am led to believe is progress.

O

History is a crutch for amnesiacs remembering to remember. The readiness with which we let go of our bitterness and move on says much about our character and capacity to forgive past injustices. I've been taught how to forgive, but I was raised by strong Chinese women who also know a thing or two about reminding you of the past. Strong Chinese women don't let you get away with silence.

O

What strength lies in *good* when *good* is a proxy for *under control*?

What use is control when just one step into water leaves you changed?

O

Stereotypes … but make it fashion! Wear this look day to night, week to month, year to grave. And repeat. And recycle. I didn't think they'd notice if I changed into something less traditional—if I kept moving to avoid being caught out by critics and the paparazzi. It has been decades since I claimed my place but they still insist I drape my motherland's loose threads around my neck. So vogue and authentic! So chinky, so chic.

○

The curse of fashion is that everything comes back even when we bury our shame in unmarked graves. Our embarrassments will be made new again with cyclical efficiency and—surprise!—they still fit perfectly. But to dance in glass slippers is to risk walking home with bloody feet, and once again we're caught out by our desire to live life now when the past is an infernal mirror waiting for someone to ask the same selfish questions. They know the slipper fits because of the blood trail that leads to your door, not because they thought to ask you to try it on.

○

I used to think all they wanted was me to be historical trauma dressed up in contemporary costume. Stand here, look this way, hold your arm out to receive the gift of eternal misinterpretation. Despite my bravado, I'm never ready to speak up when my anger kicks me in the shins. You must take to me with your biggest, heaviest sticks. Don't let me get away with forgetting myself in either silences or anthems.

○

What is the line of sight from washing ashore with hungry nets
to a day in the sun, our bodies red and softened from the spoils
of annual leave?

Where do I have to stand to be seen?

O

It's so boring to hate what you are made up of at fifteen, but I did it anyway for sport. There was so much to play with: how every edge appeared to blur into something unloveable, or how the inflections in my voice seemed to render me lesser. There are only so many ways you can regurgitate your own past before it is served back to you as your present. We call it memory loss. We call it finding other suns to hook and bury.

O

The opposite of peace is fire with a hero complex. Every time I tell the story of how we've never had the chance to really know peace for ourselves, the flames dance higher and the cracks spit louder. I can also tell you the story of how we got here: first, by waka—then boats, ships, planes, and clauses that allow for safe passage and protection. Land and blood were taken—some years were erased. Through Yellow Peril and civil war. Playground taunts that went unchecked. Thorns passed off as harmless jokes or 'satire'. Being taught that different is dangerous. More blood taken—more years erased.

O

Sometimes I've felt trapped by what I've been told I can't achieve. They ask more of me, but I'm just a man in a cape who dreams of flight—tempted by the sky's view of the world—marvelling at my shadow cast onto the scene below. I walk out into the war, my boots filled with dirt to remind me what I am made of and what I will become. This is what I'm reduced to—all because the sky never returns my calls and I'm too impatient to sit still.

○

My power grows each time one of our brothers or sisters is dragged into the news lifeless (assuming a body has been recovered) or as it did when every headless torso on a dating app assured me that they weren't racist—it was just their 'personal preference'.

○

I've eaten the words you told me I couldn't say. I've torn them from your hands with my savage teeth and shredded them, swallowed them, then spat them back out as an unapologetic F. U. I've eaten them all with chicken feet, fermented tofu and glossy black eggs raised from ash. I've let fire and water ruin your lucky days with their thoughtless ways. This is just to say: I do not apologise for my hunger and its violent needs. This is my way of showing gratitude for being allowed to bathe in refrigerator light. You always said you like being lied to, and I am always so willing to oblige. Nothing can be returned to its rightful owner without some trace of resentment.

○

THEM & US

What are *WE* but the counterweight to an admission of guilt
wherein I hide my hands when I talk?

What are *THEY* but a wrong foot forward and the fear
of being eclipsed by a brighter star?

O

I'm not here to deny a white poet their place on the shelf—I'm
here to slip my voice into their ear just to see which weapon they reach for.

O

Contrary to popular belief, no one has the ability to shape the
world into what we need to survive. Perhaps this is our collective fault
for giving in too easily to the ones with hammers and following their
instructions for how to be free. I can't remember the last time someone
told me to look to them for guidance without it being about them.

O

I've catastrophised my own hopelessness until I lost count of
the number of times I've lived through the end of the world. There is
no formula for an alternative happy ending when the world expects the
black man to be killed off first or when the gay B. F. F. is denied love and
happiness despite having the best lines and costumes. There are only
stereotypes to break open until your subversive, progressive plot twists
result in 1-star reviews on IMDb.

O

Do we measure success by a victor's accumulation of other people's heirlooms or when there is nothing left to desecrate?

O

The future inherits and loses everything—it is both executor and beneficiary. Imagine how full our museums will be when the revolution is over—imagine all the storage required for both protest signs and burning crosses. We'll stand behind safety glass or invisible rope and be taken by the desire to touch the past, if only to prove to ourselves, 'I remember that country'.

O

There is no calm if the storm never passes—no chance of rebuilding if our ruins are still warm to the touch. Eventually I must turn away from the water and find my way back in the dark. I hand my trust over to what's to come, knowing it has every right to make a fool of me. Nevertheless, I return for virtue and grace, to light a way back from the poisoned tips of grief. I return to show my fellow mythologies that I will never forget their demise. I return to claim their stars as rightful owner.

O

I'm ready now.

Stability (Version)

What I am is two boxes   checked with two fat ticks
        but still not diverse enough
only history repeating in an auditorium too small for history lessons
so I think   I might be bold enough, smart enough, worthy enough,
loved enough, in the middle enough, soft like an exposed belly
plenty to go on with making
a small incision at the base of my spine to prove I'm human enough,
mature enough to buy a house, grow up, grow wiser, grow tall enough
to reach the invitation on
        the top shelf   even though it feels like I'm
not Chinese enough
        (even with a father born in Hong Kong),
not Kiwi enough
        (even with a mother born in Lower Hutt),
not scared enough to say so, to say
        this can't be happening, shouldn't be happening,
not under my watch, under my feet the worms don't think
about whether they are early enough   to miss the birds, satisfied
        in their place,
        enough enough,
        hot enough, MASC enough, femme enough,
water running backwards on another planet, faith in a fair world restored
enough, young enough   emerging from the ocean with a perfect
beach body, not too far gone enough, kind enough to keep them close, mean
enough to keep them wanting   and still I think my voice
isn't loud enough to drown them out,   not sharp enough
to make them back down,   a tidal song,   a crowbar's reprieve
        as great-grandson facing the same demons, as son,
        brother, lover, friend,

treated as if I can't   make my mind up, can't slow down,
         can't outpace the pack,
doing my best to keep my reflection in the mirror truthful
and all this time   all these years spent   walking in the shadow of
     the past   I ask to be present enough,
stable enough to know   I'm making the right choices, the right noises
even when   the empty box still misses my name, still tells me
     I'm not enough
and so   what I am is a man looking   to the past
      asking it to release its grip   and start anew.

Identity theft for the end of the world

Your porn name is the name of your childhood pet + the first street you lived on. Your Hollywood name is the make of your first family car + a shard of glass. Your death metal band name is your greatest fear + the last thing you watched die. Your poet name is the beginning of time crackling in the air + a pearl in your shoe. Your self-portrait is five times the size of the largest lake + the divers who get lost finding their way up. Your cause of death is the harried look white people give you before deciding which seat to take on the bus + exhaustion. Your medication is a parachute in an electrical storm + the realisation that the drugs are slowly killing you. It's easier to feign belief in a world where your birth name is heavy enough to sink a boat or has a meaning that crosses languages. It's not a controversy until your name is a magnet + full-page curses in the newspaper. Your name is dirt in this town, but a golden ticket in another. Replace all canned laughter on TV with a father's regrets and reframe all the violence on the news as a makeover montage. Buy a new name in monthly instalments and prepare yourself for strange looks once you realise you can stop thinking about being good and start speaking in motion detectors. Your way back into belonging is your porn name + your Hollywood name + your poet name + all your other names written on the back of an envelope then burned in your backyard while the townsfolk watch on, their hands wrapped around each other's throats. Remember, it's not courage if it's survival. When the fire dies, seize your chance to address them and welcome them to your new name, complete with its brand new motive. Tell them, *Hello! I'm here to haunt you.*

謝 — I'm sorry I'm a Chris Tse

My name attracts confusion—an unfamiliar jigsaw piece in the mouth for some, a mistaken identity for others. I get messages intended for The Other Chris Tse, a spoken word poet and motivational speaker from Canada. The Other Other Chris Tse is also a doctor, a personal trainer, Cassandra's dad, and a blockchain specialist. Personal Trainer Chris Tse is often tagged into tweets meant for me, and at a wedding someone mistook me for Dr Chris Tse, accusing me of not recognising my fellow med school classmate. In one of The Other Chris Tse's most well-known poems he says, 'you are the same as me—just a fucking human being'. We're all the same, and every time we get mistaken I want to scream, 'I'm sorry I'm a Chris Tse'.

O

Let me put the *Chi* in Chinese—far-flung

light that knows its own name in search of

a place to land.

O

My memory closes around the heat of someone else's childhood summer—sweat-drenched T-shirts tossed onto the pavement and the chorus of the neighbourhood children's names called out from apartment windows. *It's time to come inside; it's time to eat.* Praise the name as a form of time travel—a single breath of past, present, and future. Or praise it as a long exposure—lives put to faces blurring towards a ghostly release, asking each bearer to recognise themselves.

◯

There is no reason you can't

crave both a very specific future and

a past you wish you could call your own.

◯

Nowhere in my name does it say I'm eternally blood-locked to an ancient rage that waits patiently, wanting a way into my patterns. And yet, when I was eleven, I argued with a teacher who tried to tell me how to pronounce my name, refusing to give me the benefit of identity. I can't not dwell on this tussle every time someone questions why my family's pronunciation differs from another 謝 they know. Effort is a currency some refuse to deal in; their pettiness robs those of us who rely on it in the smallest of actions.

◯

Has it always been

a resentment of

my own making?

◯

I ask myself what it is that I have no fear in leaving behind, and the balance sheet raises no alarm. I do not wither—I do not decline—I do not refuse—I do not suffocate from an expectation or assumption that I'll ever be any more than what I'm capable of being. It's everything and nothing at the full-stop of the very last line.

O

Which is to say

every act of denial

can be transformed and

politicising my resentment

is simply putting

another survival technique

through user testing.

O

One day I'll accept I can plant myself in the name of my father and find solace between ink strokes that merge to forge meaning—tug at the thread and unravel the red velvet curtain that separates *speech* from *body* from *thumb*. I'm named after my father in two languages. How do I give thanks for a gift I must carry for the rest of my life? The answer is found somewhere in protection, but for the longest of years I couldn't be certain who or what I was protecting it from.

Bilingual

Re-learning a language with a rock
    in my mouth—the slow back

and forth as I think in different
    lives—translation being a taste

of the oldest past, further back than
    what the first word can contain

insomuch as any singular, abandoned
    definition is a spark that makes it stick.

When, then? In a way it's the rote that
    prevails, syllables in mutual repetition,

building blocks compressed into presence.
    Then, when a manner of speaking is the

fortuitous hook charged with getting me
    across the line, repeatedly, volley at

the net, I still find myself mumbling
    in English as I 拜山 at

my grandparents' graves with well wishes
    and requests for guidance.

One bow.
Two bows.
Three bows.

I only make do with patterns, the far
         reach and the distant hand closed

around what I can't find the words for—
      far, closed, distant, shut—and so on

until I give up trying or someone stops listening
      and we go back to watching the news.

Four hours ahead in Aotearoa, I watch
      the past and the future unravel on television.

O

In Hong Kong the protests are the crack of a
      thousand umbrellas calling forth their own storm

and it's clear the language of anger and revolt
      is the same wherever there is something

to protect. The protestors' signs make it clear:
      Use Cantonese in Hong Kong.

My other tongue—the one used for ordering
      蝦餃 and asking about the weather—

my other tongue has a radical power? In English,
      my name rhymes with 'peace', and in Cantonese

it gives thanks. A revolution is the opposite of
      peace and thanks—it's all our pleasantries set alight.

The radical began with *radicalis, radix*—
      the roots, the basics. That our modern

uprisings are rooted in supposedly
      dead languages cannot be ignored by

lawmakers with gangs on speed dial or
      government officials who refuse to listen.

I hear every word in the world shift and so
      I trade meaning for intent

wearing down the rock in my mouth
      coating each word with its hardness

until there is no longer a switch—just one swift
      movement, a brick cast in the middle of a protest.

I feel everything colliding 9424km away in
      Wellington, where the storm can't take my tongue.

Tomorrow, and tomorrow, and tomorrow

what we wanted is now wishful thinking / battleground or loose tooth / a defence mechanism or selective hearing / these days you hear every single flag raised over the divided city / tides in the wind / everything else ripped apart by sunlight / an overdue exposure / their track record with being in the right / is diminished in their haste to never be smaller / than the sharpest insult / or the loudest crowd / the streets roar and the city shakes back / revealing its pressure points / like emergency glass / like paper lanterns / like a matchstick tower built on sand / the sirens / the makeshift shields against / the authority to inflict / it's all raising a generation that thrives on revenge fantasies / sound is your first sense before entering this world / it prepares you for the roar of chaos / a motherland's heartbeat / what is safety? / it is never fearing silence / or the sound and fury within us

Mike &
Karl &
Duncan &
Martin

Every time a white man writes an opinion column bemoaning
the caps-locked hardships of being a white man

I feel myself dying in a way that hasn't been fashionable
for several centuries

like being torn apart by a velociraptor while I'm busy
discovering the meaning of life or

strapped to a torture rack because no one trusts a gaysian
with a Kiwi accent and a creative writing degree.

Why be opaque with your reckons when you can just piss
on the graves of beneficiaries

then write about it to start a public debate about the right
to piss on the graves of beneficiaries?

Maybe one day after their words have repeatedly stabbed me
in the eyes enough times   I'll die

in a more contemporary manner—a clickbait demise designed
for maximum social media engagement—

like being shot in the back while foraging for herbs
with my genderfluid friends

or a livestream of me starving to death while trying
to save for a house. I used

to dream of paradise   but paradise is too exhausting.
Nowhere is safe

from white-man hot takes screamed at you on the daily.
'BUT... NOT ALL WHITE MEN!!'

type all the white men on the internet in unison
when they should be writing *Hamlet*.

My most memorable one night stands have been white men
so I can attest to the good

some of them contribute to the world. I let them think
they were in charge as they claimed

my mouth and my body for their own histories. I didn't
even tell them where I'm *really* from.

But if only they knew the whole time I was thinking about
how I would use them

for a poem, how their dirty words are sodden gold in my ears.
I whip my head back

and forth, shaking the pardons and contradictions loose,
giving myself permission to be

aggrieved—to march onto the internet with a fist raised high
and look them in the bylines, unblinking.

Performance art for the end of the world

a crowd gathers around an empty frame suspended from the ceiling / some see the face of their saviour / others find themselves lost in a tunnel / those at the front with their chequebooks at the ready have the audacity to call it Art / they're all correct / but they're also wrong to think a price can be ascribed to something / we're only meant to talk about and not touch / the crowd is given the option to replace the frame with a mirror that only speaks the truth / like how a bowl of rotting fruit reveals bad luck or a time of death / we can accommodate the truth if we all share an understanding of what it means to be willing to lay down our weapons / long enough to notice the cracks in the ceiling / even the shortest histories take their time to course-correct / to slip against the hands that direct them / but for many in the crowd it's easier to look through nothing at a familiar than it is to stare an unknown enemy in the eyes / it's easier to carry on with letters written in invisible ink / even if they're ultimately mistaken for scrap paper / these are the thoughts that keep me up at night / the policies and quotas they hold up as progress, which I'd generously call white noise / and the realisation we all emerge from the same chaos / slamming headfirst into riot after riot / if we treated diversity panels like performance reviews maybe we'd actually get shit done / instead of slamming fingers in doors then blaming all fingers for provoking doors / heaven allegedly waits in a sky that sounds like a badly dubbed film of two angels arguing over who gets the remote / there's a correlation between a constant noise designed to soothe and a puzzle we can't put back together / the crowd asks whether we should all have a say in what deserves to be safe in the frame / I've had too many of these conversations under fluorescent lights in offices and lecture theatres / on stages before a paying audience / always running the circuit of acceptable answers in the wild clutches of self-preservation / it's like being trapped at a party that's too noisy and getting tired of explaining why your hands are always bloodied / the crowd knows what I'm talking about / give us a frame and we'll show you what a lifetime of famine looks like / even when we go to sleep with emptiness / we wake with our bodies filled with visions of every possible happening coming true

Backbreaker

their muses dance on mountain peaks wrapped in golden skins

mine are refractions   splitting like blood cells under siege

| | | | | | | | | | | |

how much before my body breaks   under the weight of collective trauma?

| | | | | | | | | | | |

as much as I can hold   in the space between living the past

and knowing the past

| | | | | | | | | | | |

as much as I can drag from the earth   lured by the promise of warmth

alive enough to raise my arm and point at a line-up of my tormentors

and still have the audacity to laugh at my own misfortunes

| | | | | | | | | | | |

for now I'm dreaming of a future that won't deny me   as much as I can crave

and therein lies my best mistake   to have truly believed

the green light means *GO*   when in reality it's my envy blinding me

| | | | | | | | | | |

for now it's the sound of a choir tearing up sheet music

      asking the audience to turn their faces to the back of the hall

        because, for some of us, to witness is to carry another's pain

| | | | | | | | | | |

as much as I can bring myself   to give away to the highest bidder

| | | | | | | | | | |

scrape my bones clean and weigh the samples   that's the past crystallising

to the point where I can't

         lift my hands to receive intervention   as if

someone would notice me here with my ribbons streaming in the wind

| | | | | | | | | | |

when they do see us   it's not for what we have earned

| | | | | | | | | | |

no matter how warm my life has been   I'm still seen as a channel for grief a soft drone carried in me over years, decades, centuries

like my kidney troubles, the probable gout, and the very high chance

that one day my heart will simply give up

| | | | | | | | | | | |

for years I thought

vulnerability was my tongue nailed to the page and asking for their help

or maybe it was letting them   take my blood despite my fear of needles

watching silently as they extracted, tasted

and made approving noises

| | | | | | | | | | | |

before I die

I want to be a heroic noise   I want to wear love and light

to be the wow now

in a circle lifted from restful sleep

| | | | | | | | | | | |

it's not enough to play subservient then turn on them in the final hour

it's not enough to chastise them for judging bodies

by tossing them from rooftops to explode at the feet of those who

      demand blood   as if blood

is the only suitable proof of clean/tainted   a payment to settle their debts

| | | | | | | | | | | |

I refuse to be the stone they cast

I refuse to be the trick of light that has them lining up to kiss my feet

      if proof is what they want

I'll open my mouth   so they never second-guess my intentions again

| | | | | | | | | | | |

fever wave   fever come loosen the untold desires in my chest

| | | | | | | | | | | |

I've been thinking about a spell to fortify the body

and what it might mean to give up safety in exchange for resilience and what amount of gold is too much when we are already dragon-sick

and what to do with the wolves at my door still scratching to be let in

| | | | | | | | | | | |

the storm-grey line between a spell and curse will be my downfall

in these uncertain times

and yet I'll follow through   if only because I have no choice but

to embrace the consequences of my determination

| | | | | | | | | | | |

they call me brave   but what use is bravery when

the call is coming from within the house

| | | | | | | | | | | |

I've been thinking about a spell for inner strength

| | | | | | | | | | | |

I have never had a spell or peach wood

to protect me   and I'm still undecided

as to whether luck and fortune

have been on my side

| | | | | | | . | | | | |

I know I can't trust my own judgement   when I can keep dancing

through smoke and haze   without passing out

to be one with the world is a wretched bar to clear

when the closeness of enemies   teaches us nothing new

a young boy's murder   begets an act of protest

begets a corporation's woke ad campaign   begets the zeroes

of a billionaire's net worth   begets art gasping for air

where there's smoke

is no longer a reliable tell

| | | | | | | | | | | |

I've been collecting evidence of my inner strength

because even the smallest branch on the tallest tree

can recount every tremor

that pulls us into the present

binding us to lines we cannot see

but could extract from our bones

if we are forced to explain

where we came from and

where we want to go

| | | | | | | | | |

The Magician—Notes on distraction

Every time I turn to see where I should be looking
I see my reflection.

○

There is so much of the world within reach
from your desk—screens within screens, and holes
within holes—tails wagging dogs, and newspapers
crying wolf.

It's tiny hammers pounding at your skin
and not knowing why you wake up every morning
covered in bruises.

It's a story so vivid you keep repeating it
as if it were yours to tell, pulling up your sleeves and
showing strangers all the new shades of blue you've
collected.

You think you know this story and who is
telling it. Don't be surprised when a door slam shuts
and you find yourself asking, *How long has that door
been there?*

○

My reflection is a magician—he tells me where to look.

○

Inside every poem is a stage with trapdoors.

Inside every poem is a smoke machine.

Inside every poem is a mirror

                    buried in the volta

and, once found and gazed upon, it shows you

what you missed as you were following the tip

of the wand.

                    O

The Magician tells you where to look, and so you look
because magic doesn't work if you don't follow
instructions. But, as a spectator, the trick is to expect
everything and nothing at the same time.
                              The trick is to
watch the wand while your left hand is behind your back
texting the revelation to your past self, so when you reach
the reveal you have seen The Magician's flourish in all
its cross-sectioned-exposed-wiring glory.
                              Look over there—
a door you've never noticed, a secret way in and out.
Anything could be placed before you undetected.

O

Of course it's been there the whole time. You've spent
your entire life with your body pushed up against
the door, but the crowd beating on the other side
is louder and demands entertainment.

O

They spend the running time convincing us it's

a levitation
without wires

and while our eyes are scanning for the slightest
quiver

we don't see them set fire to the scenery,
the strike of the match disguised by our applause.

O

With so much happening in this world
it's getting harder

to resist everything that demands my attention,
and harder to tell

what I unknowingly steal from myself when I fall
for another smokescreen.

Over here's shattered glass scattered over the pavement,
catching sunlight and

begging to be written about. I'm so taken by its symbolism
I've not noticed its tragic source.

It doesn't stop me from getting on my hands and knees to
interrogate each shard.

O

The Magician tells me sleep is the biggest distraction
of all. There's no joy

     in surrendering to the screens behind my eyes
where everything I believe to be true is a wrong memory,
an echo I've been too happy to be swallowed by.

     In the morning, everything is the same but shifted
slightly to the right—and during the night someone has
turned all your books around so their spines are now
facing the wall.

O

The whole damn time

                              there,

          smoking away.

                    O

From the wings

both The Magician and the audience

become the show—passing

the matches between them, call and

response running in both directions.

Can we still call this power?

And, if so, how many walls

will be left standing

when they've extinguished

the flames?

O

It's from the wings that I see what haunts me.
Ignorance won't save me, no matter how many
doors I open and shut just to keep myself busy.

O

My reflection and I want to look away—but the wires snap
us back each time.

O

If you are a person of colour, you don't get to live
through a national conversation about racism and
shame without taking multiple hits to the body.

It's like being a prop in your own story and constantly
wondering whether someone will pick you up just to
acknowledge that you're there. It's screaming *FIRE!*

in a burning building while everyone on Twitter is
saying it's not fire but a smoke machine doing what
it's designed to do. A blind man doesn't need to *see*

a fire to know the rush of standing in a burning
building, and if he stands there long enough he will
be taken by the flames. So much debate rests on

the cause of the fire but no one ever wants to talk
about the consequences of making the cause the story.
Who is telling this story? Well, it depends on whether

or not you mention the colour of the bodies they'll pull
from the debris. Sometimes we have to tell these stories
because the rest of the world is watching The Magician

disappear an invisible elephant that was never there
in the first place. And behind the door you never noticed,
a series of doors. That is the story you should be telling.

O

I see my reflection
every time I turn to see where I should be looking.

In denial

Sometimes you can't tell the sky
apart from the hills—the more
you look, the more you begin to
doubt that either exists. When you're
busy arguing about the branches
dipping over your fence, you forget
it's the roots you need to tend to.
Every silent disc played on repeat
is heard light years away. When we
turn to look backwards we see it all
unfolding like a map we refuse to trust.
History is violence—kindness erased like
a weed. It's like art that moves us yet
we know we can't enjoy—a bloody knife
protruding from a portrait of a young gay man
beaten to death. No gentle shades of
watercolour—just black vivid scrawled
on a bus shelter screaming at us to leave, or die.

Abandoned acceptance speech for outstanding achievement by a Chinese New Zealander in the field of excellence

Thank you!   Thank you!   多謝晒, you impressionable bastards!
It's an honour to stand here on the edge of this melon-green sea
with the foam seeping through my bespoke vegan leather sandals
feigning surprise to have received this in such a competitive year
of excellence by Chinese New Zealanders, some of whom I'm not
related to.

I applaud my fellow nominees. I've been in your position before,
and let me tell you that tonight your mattress may feel like a sack
of bricks as you struggle to comprehend this loss. I too have
struggled with the shame of desiring a validating slap on the back
while everyone else suffers from delusions of adequacy. Your time
will come, as mine has tonight.

To receive this award is to receive a kiss from a drunken angel.
The smell of your putrid congratulations will cling to me for days;
I take great comfort in knowing that some will point and stare
when they realise I am the source of their unease. The path to this
moment hasn't been smooth—in fact, it's been booby-trapped
like a *Home Alone* film directed by the makers of *Saw*.

There have been sacrifices; there have been compromises.
But most of all, there have been awkward silences when I joke
about eating dogs in a room of my Caucasian peers, who clutch
their wine glasses tighter and don't know whether to laugh or
call the SPCA.

I'll be the first to admit that I've done some things I'm ashamed of
to get to where I am today. It was what it was the day I decided
to change my name to John Smith to see whether my calls would
finally be returned, and it is what it is, this circling of reasons,
my achievements assessed and judged by a jury with no longing
for the taste of something wild, something that knows how to
retaliate when attacked.

Life is the cruellest joker because it doesn't fear the consequences
of its actions—that's the only way I can explain how I find myself
to be standing here before this radiant audience of my peers while
another, more violent, crowd outside this theatre jostles like
Boxing Day shoppers waiting for the mall doors to be flung open.
I can already smell the blood marinating the air. They have been
so generous with their attempts to destroy me, to teach me a lesson
about personal growth.

In hindsight, I should've reacted with more indignation to their taunts,
perhaps organised a riot or two, but even fireworks have off days when
the sky is clouded over, or there's an unexpected whale in the harbour
we don't want to spook. I thank you for this award, and see it as your
attempt to not spook me.

However, tomorrow, when the day is reset and this moment has
been immortalised as a self-deprecating yet earnest social media
post, I'll go back to being an unironic plastic Buddha in a souvenir
shop next to the Mao bobbleheads and calligraphy sets.

No one else will remember this night and what it means to me.
The spotlight, with its selective amnesia, will find another face similar
to mine to bathe in adoration. The sky will regretfully inform me it has
no room for another star, that the empty expanse I see was reserved
centuries ago by people with the right names and faces.

I thank you for giving me this moment rather than tossing my
honey-coated body from the roof of this theatre into the crowd outside.
If I could only describe how blinding the lights are from this side
of the stage, how I can't bear to look directly into what I can only
assume is a feeling of knowing there is a place for me.

Now that I've seen my name etched in gold, everything else is a
punchline that hurts to laugh at. If that isn't success, I can't imagine
what else I could do besides scream until my lungs pop. Don't you see?
We're all winners! And this is our shared reward for pretending that
everything's fine.

So, once more, thank you—this award means more to me than
I'll ever admit to myself. I leave you now with a reason to go on.
I leave you with a promise to destroy what has been built over
the bones of our forgotten accomplishments, as a measure of
my appreciation.

Vexillology

A flag

'A flag with six colours of the rainbow, generally including red, orange, yellow, green, blue, and purple.'

— Emojipedia entry for 'Rainbow Flag'.

A flag with six parts with which to assemble the perfect specimen, or a set of principles to enrich the soul. A flag with no defined end, save for the pot of gold that is promised to us when it allegedly gets better.

A flag with six histories denied entry to the party, generally on the grounds of homophobia, transphobia, sexism, racism, misogyny, and miscellaneous fuckery attributed to those who are in and those who want out.

A flag of six dares at a teenage party, generally including kisses, nudity, stolen road cones, setting fire to bags of shit, prank calls, and (in the meta horror film version) the disposal of a body.

A flag of six new cautions for old misadventures; an old flame's laugh in a crowded bar; a misheard instruction; dried blood on barbed wire; friends circling back to strangers; sunburn under your lips; a joke about murder.

A flag of six unpopular facts disseminated through social media, generally designed to deny us the chance to buy a vowel, reject authority, wrestle with trolls, dig up past grievances, destroy reputations, and prove chaos.

A flag with six stripes discarding colours of the past. There is no pride in letting names fade away while others gaze lovingly at an unreachable sky. Why do we give in to clichés when there is so much to grow from?

first, light / then memory / then accusation / then remedy / then recovery
/ and, finally, slowing down / until the mountain you've climbed no longer
resembles land / but a shadow you look past / in order to see light again

spoke about this in front of a crowd / clicks, cheers, applause / whoop for us
faggots in the streets / because some trust / I have it in me to use all three of
my voices: / loud, louder, loudest / when I holler I surprise myself

each kiss became a scar / I grew to hate my body / the cones are still in my
parents' garage / the fire spread to the streets / we're all too scared to answer
our phones / I found the grave by following the scent of aniseed

when seen askew / you could say the breakthrough / is to teach a new dog
old tricks / make tradition a comfort to aspire to / despite knowing that the
process / will leave a trail of destruction / they'll question our methods

they'll say I'm imaginary / to seed doubt about my legitimacy / one more nail
in the coffin won't hurt / if I'm not expected to rise to the occasion / yes it's a
guessing game / that no one can win / unless you hold the hammer

never end with a question if you don't expect an answer / I've gone
unanswered / for nearly 40 years / we found ways to turn / six, eight colours /
into a single idea / in order to ask you must be prepared to listen

(Hot pink—Sexuality)

I told myself repeatedly / foolishly / I would never be the same / unhooking

my body / from beneath the rapturous sun / to toss it unceremoniously into

a psychedelic sea / of abandoned youth and nets for dial-up beefcake / begging

for a way out before I'd even found the way in / my golden ticket promised

only disappointment / no flesh raised for claiming / I teased their lines and sought

invitations to any parties willing to relieve me / from the pain of hiding in plain

sight / I made purity a weakness / some starve the same hungers / some choose

to succumb / I was was stuck on repeat / no different from anyone else on fire

O

I fucked a man who refused to say my name / it kept me from being a part of

his shame / I could've been a plot twist or a direct line of action / like a hammer to

a nail / there is no shame in being the nail / in being the steel that joins and holds

two bodies together / there is no shame in being the hammer / wielding its force /

its bloody consequences bound in the pink of broken flesh / a flood will come to

wash it away / everything slicked back / like the earth I'll be undone / reset

so I can eat up / fold my tongue into another man's skin / take from his sweat and

cum / the stories I'll need / to sustain a lifetime of dirty dreams / no meal is clean

O

an easy intrusion / pin as point / prick—but no token piercing / that's why

skin / being layered sheets / is no greater at containment / than the staunchest

wall built with confidence / assuaging keen fear / taunting those predators

circling the fortress, hungry / but that one pin asks blood to spill / whether

boy has danced with risk in his nights / the vastness of the universe / cannot

compete with what this single drop has to say / the result is its own master /

an aftermath rolling through his head / collecting every / what if / what now

and what will I do when the angels sing / their broken wings / shadowplay

(Red—Life & Courage)

In one life, you're the aftermath of a dental hygiene appointment gone
wrong and I'm the minimum wage worker cleaning up the mess with
tiny toothbrushes. Sometimes you're Holden Caulfield hogtied in
someone's boot and I'm a souped-up Holden Commodore with a
subwoofer so ferocious everyone in the traffic jam shits their pants.
True courage is recognising your teenage heroes were all monsters
and instructing the fire to take you all down in the spectacular swell
of an orchestral score punctuated with tasteful dubstep drops.

○

Learn to live with your own discomfort, to unshackle your hang-ups
and enter every all-staff meeting with the confidence of an anti-vaxxer
sharing 'research' on Facebook. We just want to leave the comfort of our
houses in the morning fully formed like a baby born in a Hollywood film:
spotless and definitely not covered in someone else's insides. You too
can cruise supermarket aisles pressing jars of pasta sauce to your cheeks
without a care in the world, whispering Fiona Apple lyrics as a mantra.
The glass warms to your touch and the sauce within blooms in agreement.

O

Describe how it feels, speeding towards a doom of your choosing.
This only works if *doom* is an acceptable synonym for *living*, and
choosing to be happy is a form of activism. It's worth it when your
choices are rewarded with the velvety caress of the Cowardly Lion
swooning at your feet. There's no weakness in admitting that you're
afraid of the dark—no need to shiver when a shadow passes through.
Describe the ideal future that comes to mind as you step across the
threshold, ready to sell your life story for a medal you haven't earned.

'This is the golden age of something good and right and real.' — Taylor Swift ('State of Grace')

(Orange—Healing; visions of possibilities)

I take the key to eternal youth and bury it in the past. || My blood is slow. ||

I take half a pink pill once a day to stop my body from attacking itself.

I take the other half the next day to remind my body to stay on my side.

I take seven clean sheets of paper and make a week out of nothing.

I take the old nothing and rest it against the time I now have at hand.

I take the cracked skin on my hands as evidence of my full potential.

I take my curses and drop them into the mouths of my little demons.

I take apart the sun and build myself another world. || My blood is fast. ||

O

Someone tell me when to jump. Set five alarms spaced three minutes

apart. Sound a klaxon or bring back life-affirming noises of yesteryear:

horses bleating as they stare into their futures in frozen lakes; the sun

cracking; the photocopied moon whispering to its replicas. I can't tell

you what's going to happen next—but you knew I was going to say that

before the words magnetised in my brain. Round here, we see much more

than we're willing to confess—our dreams and visions are the safety nets

into which we tumble when our greatest ideas turn out to be dangerous.

O

On summer nights I walk to the water, but despite needing its reassurance

to calm me I hesitate to dive in. Instead, I huff lungfuls of fresh salty air to

prove my presence, setting my body in time with whatever force or deity has

the ability to bring the sky down to give answers to us hopeful fools. It's not

courage I'm looking for—that would be lazy. And it can't be faith if I don't

believe in such avenues. We all wait for signs to mend the parts of us we've

neglected, then wait for a correction if the remedy turns to blame. Open a story.

Close a story. I have so much to let go—I fear the water can only take so much.

(Yellow—Sunlight)

Time is the shroud we can't clean. It paralyses me—the thought of its
filth pressing on my body, filling and emptying me in equal measure.
When the world burns we take her ashes into our lungs. We learn to
inhabit the end, which is nothing but a prolonged process hijacking
our senses like the hesitating drag of rusty saw teeth across the frame
that holds the sky up. I had no choice but to shake hands with time;
now I look up to the sun and ask for it to sing to me, make me clean.
There is no telling if I will be lifted or burnt by its disinterest in me.

○

I've grown accustomed to this body by leaning into the spaces it desires
to fill. It's surprising what the body can do with violence dressed up
as pleasure—that satisfaction can come from pain suggests sometimes
what is meant to be shut out deserves our consideration. We return to
heated comfort every time—how is it any different from leaving a window
open during a storm and walking in to find a changed terrain? There is
a thrill in expansion. On Mars, time would have to slow down or pause
to stay in sync. Everything turns; everything is busyness in parentheses.

O

Every day I consider what's worth memorialising with the patterns we call language, especially when we're constantly reminded that there is nothing new under the sun. We are our own questionable narrator—we can't not believe there is a season worth waiting for, instead of years spent crawling under houses because the previous tenants stashed a fortune to bribe their way out of the impending civil war. But what I know now to be true is how everything is darker in broad daylight, especially when the old clashes with the new to reckon with our need for resolution. Fastest to supernova wins.

'The world is turnin'. I hope it don't turn away.' — Neil Young ('On the Beach')

(Green—Nature)

This is a poem about waterfalls, and the solitary drop that starts it all.

This is a poem about turning 36 in an Icelandic gay bar with a pint in

one hand and a bag of free dinner rolls in the other, and not knowing

whether what I feel is a harmony of home or a saga I have compelled

myself into believing is my blood song. My traitor heart; my fickle feet.

I can so easily put aside my mistrust of water whenever I'm taken by

its exquisite roar. For everyone back home, it's just water. For me, it's

the will of nature—to go where it must. This is a poem about moving.

O

The mantra is that green is the pinnacle of purity, but this isn't always

the case. I'm 100 per cent sure we're draining the natural world of meaning.

My response to landscapes used to be that there was too much of every-

thing and I didn't have the patience to let it be or to simply be. Then there

was Iceland. Now I ask for every vista to ruin me so I can always see the

world with new eyes untampered by expectation. See—I'm such a damn

liar. Even with my new sight I expect something to make me feel alive, as

if this is all a picturesque waterfall is good for. Enough can be too much.

O

On the night of my 36th birthday I looked up and there was the aurora

swimming above us. Pannett, Erin and I tried to catch it on our phones but

our hands were too slow or not slow enough. Such charmless praise to say

a place has changed you when you are constantly changing, but how do

you escape something you've run towards? I could be the boy in the saga

destined to be both tyrant and poet. Destiny—the force that pushes us

towards something meant to be, whether real or unimaginable. Now and

then I forget the sky isn't always electric. I forget how to change back.

(Turquoise—Art & Magic)

Rothko Chapel, January 2014

1. A room in which my hushed mind was a kaleidoscope waiting for light.

2. I thought about the past year and the absences I allowed to fill me.

3. I thought I'd never rid myself of the intimacy that pained my heart.

4. The three words I'd later use to caption the moment: calm, peace, shadow.

5. Memory tells me I saw black, but each passing year leaves me in doubt.

6. Rothko said colour is 'merely an instrument' for expressing emotion.

7. I've spent my life ascribing too many meanings to every bloom and blush.

8. There were times I thought I'd die under the weight of a rainbow.

O

Len Lye Centre, January 2017

1. Every line jumps like tiny thunder caught in a frame.

2. Crushed jazz—metallic growl—people falling in together after disaster.

3. Paint like blood that's been asked to give away the world's secrets.

4. I find myself backing away from every screen that knows too much.

5. I used to think meaning existed between capture and disappearance.

6. That the way we allow ourselves to be overcome by colour is human.

7. I worry that I've been conditioned, perhaps softened, by its frequencies.

8. I have to ask myself why I consider that to be such a bad thing.

O

Olafur Eliasson, Tate Modern, October 2019

1. The surrounding light drains us; we become monochrome.

2. But in the big room we are split into our separate shadows.

3. The spectrum still dances when no one is looking. It is always alive.

4. The bridge between art and magic is an eye looking through a prism.

5. What I know to be art can only be explained by the thumping in my chest.

6. And the stillness in my blood. And the undoing of how I view water.

7. Looking up is the only way I'll see the whole—the hoop that holds our gaze.

8. Even a black sphere casts colour when it is opened up just so.

(Indigo—Serenity)

Sometimes we dance alone in our living rooms to hard songs after
the world has tossed us out onto pavements to fend for ourselves.
Sometimes the song is too soft, so we throw open our windows and
bargain with the night to toughen our edges. Try the night with your
vision impaired. Try the night with a side of marketable trauma—make
blood the ornamental centrepiece of your living. Grief is performance
as much as it is tempering their expectations of you being Goldilocks
until they find you sleeping in their beds without a care in the world.

○

Breathe when you are randomly selected at the airport for an explosives test.
Breathe when you are your own story and they threaten to erase you.
Breathe when you are the frontrunner in a neverending race.
Breathe to darken blood and fortify throats with anthems.
Breathe through burning crosses and violent silences.
Breathe in technicolour and black and white.
Breathe in ampersands and ellipses.
Breathe yourself inside out.

O

I carry on but I also carry an inky blur behind my eyes that warns me when I'm trying too hard to be normal. It reminds me to place faith in whatever the negative is empowered to inhabit, that the opposite of chaos doesn't necessarily have to be calm. Let me be the exotic ethnic to your iPhone Notes apology for cultural appropriation. Let me be the Number One Dime to your Scrooge McDuck. I'll put my pain on show if it means I get to swim in a sea of gold coins as a reward. This is the result I am after: the ability to defy physics for an improbable poetic image. I know I can be golden too.

(Violet—Spirit)

I want them to see me for a double: one on the inside tending to

ashen walls, the other feeding the bonfire outside. My left hand

won't shake my right hand won't shake the mirror won't shake

the other left hand. Both have held on for so long it's impossible

to tell what is reflection and what is imagined. I used to think

I would suit the martyr, back when my voice held the shape of

being unsolved and senseless. Now I can tell them they were

wrong to doubt me; it was always in my interest to be so bold.

O

Screens are mirrors—a way to show that which we are made of,

beyond atoms, moving parts and the lists of pros and cons we use

to determine what is worth starting a movement over. Ask yourself:

how am I seen and by whom? Screens demonstrate blood as utility,

flesh as construction. The truth's other side is that screens lie faster

than they can comfort—they crush dreams, set the die off course

and force the fit that leaves us scratched up. All I want is a pattern

I can relate to—something like symmetry without the call for order.

O

I've fumbled through their terms and conditions in high resolution

knowing I'm made up of many stereotypes, but even after earning

permission to call myself a poet, I still can't tell which ones are real.

If an ant can pass the mirror test, I have no excuses—but the part of

me that recognises the scars on my back deserves an apology. What

I see can't be captured—it's the reason I spin in circles, waiting for

the earth to fall away. Even when our rituals become requisite we

never stop to question the need for filling a room with dying flowers.

Poetry to make boys cry

Identikit

when asked to explain the lines that lead to now, you describe /
the shape of your body as it hits water / the shape of cold water
shocking muscle / the shape of fleshy chambers forced to loosen
and acquiesce / the shape of your grandparents in their coffins /
the shape of coffins that are too small to contain entire lifetimes /
the soft and hard moments we can't forget no matter how often we
turn our backs to the light / [you write this poem out of love / but
even love can be a blindfold] / the shape of you and your parents
standing in your grandparents' driveway / after being kicked out
for talking to your aunty's white boyfriend / your hand reaching
out to someone you don't recognise in a dream / their silhouette
branded upon your brain / [you've tried to swallow the night and
all its inhabitants / but they weren't designed for consumption] / the
night standing in for doubt / as you argue with your own memory /
waking up to the smell of 皮蛋瘦肉粥 / the shape of a bowl designed
to hold love / love that is never spoken of because to do so would
silence it / the shape of silence when you tell your parents you've
fallen in love with a white boy / the shape of that white boy pressed
against your body / both your hearts / shaped like hungry mouths /
the shape of your mouth biting into the world's biggest egg / the
shape of years spent running before walking / your knees shredded
and bloody / even after you grew the thick skin they said you would
need in this lifetime / the years pass like a watched pot / but you imagine
steam rising from its wide open body / flashbacks to the shape of air
being forced into a lifeless body / some incisions are made to clean

blood, others to fast-forward a certain end / when your grandparents
spoke of life it was whatever came their way / no one back then had
time to hide behind the sky / to pull strings / to taste control / the shape
of control does not fit with the shape of effort / a grounded bird tries
to climb an invisible ladder to heaven / to correct a path the world
wouldn't let it look upon / in case it traced a line too close to comfort /
we all fear the shape of comfort when it belongs to someone else /
forgetting that we all look the same buried six feet under / both your
grandparents appear before you on the night you learn how to take off
your blindfold / when you finally recognise the shape of acceptance /
and how it might fit among the ruins of your rejections / it goes like this: /
the fights, the kisses, the direct hits / unfolding yourself into a shape
the world doesn't know how to contain / what doesn't fit / what doesn't
hold true / the shape of your name / the shape of a bowl that never
empties / all of these things fit together if you turn them the right way up /
you run your finger along the lip of the bowl and remember / what it
means to be laced in time and not know how to use your hands to feed
yourself / you count the years / you feel their shape flooding your
throat / making a noise / making a space for what's to come

Love theme for the end of the world

He thumbs me like the *Oxford Dictionary* until he finds what he's looking for. To find the definition of love, the eyes must hover over every new feeling before moving on.

○

The first time he broke my heart I thought he was rejecting what I meant to him. 'Love is pain—oh, oh, oh!' sang Girls Aloud on *Out of Control* (2008), their last album before taking a hiatus, which is pop music euphemism for breaking up. It's good to see yourself in pain even if you refuse to believe that's what your voice really sounds like, even if you refute that shadow cast over your face in the last photo of the two of you taken together as together.

○

We can make sense out of anything if we're given enough time—enough for two to find their way back to each other to invent a word and keep it between them. My scattershot approach to loving him was pulling apart every half-finished love poem until I found what I was looking for: meaning where there was no meaning, or our history reduced to a thousand papercuts.

○

My favourite type of gay porn is when two men talk about their day and nobody dies. When I was fifteen the internet moved like honey—slow but with a sweet return. Nowadays, frustration is a photo of two men holding hands censored by Instagram. I know porn isn't the best place to find love, but I don't always have the time to shave and iron a shirt. He irons my shirts; he doesn't shave. I wonder what he'd look like without a beard, so he shows me photos of himself when the internet wasn't around for us to look back at our past selves. I'm too scared to tell him that his is the only photo on my phone when I look at my future self.

○

I wonder about the end of the world and whether it would be reason enough to give up on love, or if it is in fact the reason we should keep banging on about it. I wonder if a heartless body can learn to keep loving. I wonder if knowing the meaning of now will be enough to prepare me to embrace tomorrow.

○

When 公公 taught me how to use a dictionary he explained how it was for more than just learning how to spell a word. Here were all the meanings of the world in my hand; I felt so powerful holding such nourishment. Every time I see my parents they ask if I've eaten before sending me home with enough meals for the rest of the week. Dad moved to New Zealand to start a new life knowing only my mum. I never assumed courage could be inherited, but sometimes I can't bear to be in a room surrounded by people I know and love. And so is love—too bright to look in the eye, too bright to ignore.

What's fun until it gets weird?

There are no winners when you play Cards Against Humanity with your mum.

There are no winners when you have to explain what smegma is or the mechanics of a glory hole. You have opened a door you cannot close—you have lit the fuse of a truth bomb so great your childhood is now raining down around you like confetti at a public execution, like wigs at a drag queen graduation. When you witness how surprisingly good your mum is at this game of awfulness, you'll wonder whether her naivety and innocent questions are all for show. What if she's trolling you? What if this is payback for all the awkward questions you asked her as a child? Perhaps she has never forgiven you for breaking into a haka at a pedestrian crossing because a Māori man was also waiting to cross. Even though the son responsible for that particular public embarrassment was your brother, she's reached the point where all of the stupid things you did as kids can and will be attributed to either one of you.

There is no excusable justification for a family bonding activity that involves your mum and your aunties cackling over the phrase 'Fucking a corpse back to life' and then winking at each other across the table, as if to say, 'These kids have no idea'. You and your cousins will look at each other and with your cousin telepathy—which is similar to a WhatsApp group chat only more exhausting because you can't turn off notifications—you'll all think-say to each other, 'Whose fucking idea was this? Don't you dare leave this table, Shannan, we're making this memory together.'

We all thought this would be a good idea, perhaps even fun, but then every good idea gets corrupted sooner or later. Every good idea is a meme ruined by the Young Nats. Every good idea has a secret past involving a shotgun wedding and/or snakeskin pants. Every good idea has the potential to kill you in your sleep.

There is no turning back once you've played the 'bukkake' card. From this moment, your days will be ice cream melting on pavements and bone fragments in vegan pies and the image of your mum getting ready for bed reaching for her Estée Lauder night cream will make you wish you'd thought twice about playing that damn card. From this moment, the world will be a Lynchian nightmare of backmasked beat poetry and a VHS loop of your mum chanting 'bukkake, bukkake, bukkake' while scooping mayonnaise out of a jar with her hands and feeding it to your neighbour's dog Sparky.

There is no time to be embarrassed or vague when you explain these things to your mum because the alternative is that she'll turn to Google, and you have no idea what the safe search settings are on her work computer. It's probably best that she hears it from you. This is one of your unspoken responsibilities as a child, along with setting up your parents' wireless printer and finding a restaurant for dinner that caters to your dad's terrible luck with car parking, your mum's passionate distrust of herbs and is listed in the fucking Entertainment Book.

Well—Mum, Aunties—when several men and a woman love each other—actually maybe they don't have to love each other, but they certainly should at least be good enough acquaintances that they will engage in small talk about the next kindy working bee when they run into each other in the cereal aisle—and maybe it doesn't have to be a woman—maybe it can be another man—so when several men and a woman or another man have consensually agreed to what's about to happen they have a special cuddle—OK, it's less a cuddle and more a group masturbation session—they jointly jerk off and when the men are about to finish—when the men are ready to express their love or casual acquaintance—when the men are on the edge of … ejaculating … they do so on her—or his—… face.

There is no blistering silence like the one that follows while your mum and aunties ponder this explanation before submitting their supplementary questions. You're not equipped to handle their queries about the ethics or etiquette of bukkake and what even constitutes bukkake—does there have to be a minimum number of participants? Who gets the enjoyment out of it? Because when it comes to sex and enjoyment the balance is never weighted equally, so is it the givers or the receivers who get the most out of this experience? Then your mum asks, 'Have you ever done it before?' and your life will flash before your eyes like a haunted Viewmaster—like a *This Is Your Life* montage scored by Hans Zimmer—like an out-of-body experience with puppets. Your aunties and cousins turn expectantly to hear your response. One of them has a box of popcorn and your out-of-body self will think, 'Where did Justine get that popcorn?' and before either you or your out-of-body self can comprehend what is happening you'll say to your mum, 'Well, I don't think it really counts because it was just me and one other guy and he caught me by surprise'—and shit—you made it worse. You've somehow made explaining what bukkake is to your mum and aunties worse. Then Shannan will say, 'Isn't that called a facial?' and before you can shoot her your most poison-fire-tipped death stare your mum asks, 'What's a facial?'

There is no readily available time travel science to send you back in time to slap Past Chris, the inventors of Cards Against Humanity and, while you're at it, the writer who decided that Rory should sleep with Dean, much to Lorelei's disappointment, perpetuating the narrative of Gilmore women disappointing their mothers with their sexual dalliances. There is no magic spell or brainwashing device capable of erasing the night's events. There is only a silent ride home and a hasty goodbye when your parents drop you off. There are further follow-up questions the next day via text. There are tears in the cereal aisle when Max's dad John avoids eye contact because he is far too acquainted with them and heads straight to the checkout even though he hasn't found everything he came here for so now he'll have to make a stop at the New World down the road where the gluten-free bread is more expensive but it's worth it to not have to make small-talk with you.

There are craters on Mars that were once filled with water.

There are children born to parents who have waited their whole lives to love them.

There are no winners when you play Cards Against Humanity with your mum.

The other side of the glass

I was working a sausage sizzle fundraiser on the day
George Michael died. His ghost sat with me in my car
while I scrolled through social media exploding with
grief and links to his greatest hits. George took my hand
and told me not to cry before asking why I smelt of
burning flesh.

                    'Are we in hell?' he asked.
'Lower Hutt,' I replied.   My sunburnt neck
pulsed with residual heat or perhaps it was the spark
of a memory of watching him perform at
Sydney Mardi Gras in 2010 flanked by shirtless cowboys,
leather daddies and policemen in latex pants. I think about it
all the time. Every now and then I crave that night again,
trepidation running slick down my spine every time I locked
eyes with another guy, hoping my smile would be returned
favourably. A certain beat can unlock the body heat of that
glittering night and all the other nights of careless yearning
since then tumbling from limb-crushing dancefloor into
the crisp 3 a.m. air with his voice still ringing in my ears:

  'You've got to go to the city.
      You've got to reach the other side of the glass.'

Some of us are neither sunburst nor shade but a symptom
of formative summers caught somewhere in between, like
hands pressed against the edge of the rest of our lives.
The glass was my own making and all my future wonders
were one swift and decisive thought away. I wrote
all my desires in my breath for anyone to read them.

Poetry to make boys cry

Give me your attention   and I will give you an inferiority
complex dripping in summer tears so wet   I'm incapable
of assisting during any emergency—all my limbs throwing
themselves every which way to make a moment with my nothing.
I think I've convinced myself   that a fist is all I need to be a man
or a stride wide enough to cross over into enemy territory in one step.
I apply reason to everything, as if to say to my doubters,
                                        Go tell the sea to change its colour.
Time to amputate   *I think ...*   from my sentences—time to
make my mark without softening. From now on, I raise blood
without hesitation.   Give me a reason to gorge
on the gamified gay experience   like an amnesiac at a family reunion
being tricked into changing their will   or give me a darkroom packed
so tightly all our ideas of a masculine beauty standard
have finally collapsed like a star
                        in the darkest truth of space
where there is no pain behind a night that starts with tequila shots
and ends with scrambling for seats on the last bus to Lower Hutt.
            Even when no stranger has offered up their bed or body heat
I tell myself that I'm still a man—still a thick knot at the end of a rejection
that never ceases to sting.   Mum said I'd be lonely if I came out,
but loneliness relies on context to make it something to run from.
The fact is   I was already lonely—midnight and folk music
had already claimed me.   No matter how lonely you might feel
you can still perform the Heimlich manoeuvre on yourself
with or without the aid of a stable edge.   Which is to say,
sadness is sexy if you know how to fuck around it—all you need is
something blunt to run into.   So c'mon boys—make yourselves
at home in my newfound nerve and give me the affirmation

only a firm hand wrapped around a throat can bring, the way your teeth
shatter the light in this nightclub and tell me what you're really after.
Bite hard but please don't leave a mark—don't leave evidence
of the lengths I've gone to give myself away.

It doesn't hurt to have a stranger pin you against a wall,
to fully appreciate the way that power and control can resuscitate
your fantasies.   I didn't just come here to watch daddies dance
to Carly Rae Jepsen, if you know what I mean.

I came to set traps;

I came to ruin lives.
I want someone to play along with my abrasive skin
so I'll know what it's like to touch another man and stay with them.

Do you know what I mean?

White flag

(after Grant Lingard)

I surrender my body   to all histories—
the visible and the vanished—piercing through
the afterglow of erotic waste like holes
in the tight shirts I used to wear to
attract older men.   Now they only attract moths
light-drunk and   in search of keratin. That was
me before I knew how to recognise my own hand
punching every wall in my path, skin perforated
and refusing to hold any shape—at least the ones
I considered desireable. I craved the colour black to
contain me—I shunned white because it reveals
too much when you're considered dirty. A needle
pulling thread doesn't always leave a stitch.

Buried deep on a VHS tape in our TV cabinet
was a 90s hunk   in red tartan boxer shorts
seduced by   one of his teachers. I coveted
those shorts   so I would know what it might feel like
to be desired. It didn't work—nor did the jockstraps
or the tank tops or the faux snakeskin pants
all worn for show and to tell, ultimately, nothing.
Fortune's Fool learns to simmer in vain, correcting
their course with one bloodied and bruised hand.
I know this is my body.   I know this is my refuge.
I know sometimes   I must take away
its privacy to make amends with what I was
afraid to deem plain or ornamental.

Infernally yours,
gentleman poet in the streets — raging homosexual in the sheets

Every gay is Halloween and the best-selling costume is 'sexy heterosexual'.
Peek out your aggressively conservative middle-class windows and you'll see
the gay agenda in action—Instagram thirst traps marching through your streets
demanding their share of free candy. Remember those novelty pens you tip
upside down and the clothes fall off a busty lady? Tip me upside down and
watch my skin fall at your feet, then throw my homosexual skin into a rusty
oil drum roaring with the heat of a thousand flaming queens during Pride Month.
I have survived a lifetime of designing my own private Inferno—I dare you
to take it from me. And for those of you still in doubt—OF COURSE WE HAVE
AN AGENDA! How else will smart-casual rompers become a thing?

○

If you're disgusted or questioning your own skin, I invite you to write to your MP.
Write to the internet. Write and vent until someone steps in to save us from our
collective fixation on skin—the wearing of it, its propensity for itching and infection,
its unforgiveable necessity and what we argue it stands for. Make it clear that being
named 'best dressed' means nothing when you wear your diamonds at breakfast,
that we make-believe until we make it something to obliterate. I resent nostalgia,
especially when I have a reputation to destroy. I'd rather set fire to the crown and
watch it melt, until the plastic lump in my hands is a trophy I can take to bed,
fusing with my skin overnight, a shrunken inconvenience to remind me
of every single grudge I've nurtured and slept with just to spite myself.

BOY OH BOY OH BOY OH BOY

(after Sam Duckor-Jones)

oh, boys   oh, don't do that wasteland thing
with my heart   & oh   in case you're considering it
you can love stone & clay   with the same kinetic rigour   with which
you embrace the mountains   & the thickened slip that comes to rest
between touch & feel   oh, boys
sometimes I wear myself out like an accelerator in lockdown
all speed with nowhere to go   oh, Geronimo!
what do you say about lining up in single file to marvel at each other's
crushes   in exclamation marks & deep-voiced exaltations
& asking a choir to press itself along   an orchestra tuning
to raise a riot we can wear proudly on a Saturday night at home
oh, pitch like a thick black line   oh, 440Hz
a thing harder than clay   is the mind that first thought it   oh, boys
if we could all make husbands with our own hands   & learn to love
them   without   looking   over   our   shoulders
in the dark   never ever would the world question our unison
never ever would sashaying   ·   into happiness be a mark against
our names   they'll find us in a room stacked with fluorescent vases
they'll find us swilling dry martinis   & laughing about how we used
to see dust instead of glitter   oh, happy celestial bodies
oh, dreamsome days of ohs and exes   kiss kiss, boys   kiss kiss

I am everyone's gay BFF and I've earned unfettered access to all your ruby slippers

In my poppy-induced fever dreams I am the glittering example of homosexual
support   I always knew I'd grow into.   Turns out I have the heart
to be a tin man as well as the gumption a good witch needs to cover up murder.
If only   I had the budget to licence Sixpence None The Richer
for my many makeover reveals!   It's true—I'd sometimes short-change myself
to serve someone else's self-discovery   and every night I would scrub away
my hopes and dreams   with the ashes of past tomorrows.   I thought I'd be
dead by now—I thought my time would never come.   But I got the shoes!
And soon I'll have a getaway balloon and a devoted following to back my alibi.
I wasn't there, was I?   I was off somewhere in the distance using
all my guiles to convince a racist country to love me.   He said *jump*
and I said *how high?*   He said *speak* and I said *which tongue?*   But when he said
go back to where you came from   I had to explain that particular story
doesn't exist any more—it's a phantom limb waving from a haunted TV.
See—I click my heels and nothing happens.
There's no place like the scene of a racial reckoning.   (And repeat, and repeat.)
Although they have immortalised my tormentor in exam questions and
recycled half-apologies   turns out these limp wrists can carry an axe
with the conviction of a superhero. Turns out I know how to dress up
a villain's untimely death as a musical number.   My success is your success.
My enlightenment is your cue to dismantle the power structures that perpetuate
the need to be fully formed in order to be taken seriously. I am not incomplete
without a brain   or a heart   or courage   or a home.   I can be
missing all those accoutrements and still recognise that the world is unfair
or know full well what I can bring to their false shrines. You can trust me
to stand my ground—I've survived a tornado and have the shoes to prove it.

Geometric Growth

(after Guy Ngan)

Lay the earth out in all its finery.
Among its rough tenderness is where
I'm rendered seen—
a jagged shoot   among straight lines
searching for clarity.

///

My reason for being
has been sung as a game, danced around
and, in the far reaches of our histories,
declared a spell for fortune.

///

It's not a prediction if you have a say in making
it a reality
nor is it a correction of your failures.

Perhaps it's a lock, or a key, or a measure of time
that we haven't been able to tame
leaking into the wild.

There's no clean way
for us to ask our other selves
where we came from
and why it matters that we're here.

///

I was a monument in another life:
　　a presence for all
　　a target for some.

///

If I could slip into the robe of The Creator
for a wishful moment and lay down
everything I want this world to be,
I would build:

　　/ a corner for change
　　　a corner for newspapers ruined by rain
　　　a corner for artworks that no one understands
　　　a corner for the sound of fire on a summer night /

　　\ two walls held up by thoughts and prayers
　　　the other two suspended from a crane \

　　/ a ceiling forged from the fascination
　　　of wanting to know how we all die
　　　　and where we go. \

　　///

Eventually we'll all know
   what it means to nurture an idea
      until it reaches for light

  then let it pass
       into being. We're often
  quick to define what

an edge symbolises
   forcing us all into a very
      particular way of seeing.

///

      They say: a limit. I say: scope,
      the same thing seen anew
      from different past lives

      made real only when we can
      come to an agreement that
      there is nothing to divine

      from the very abstractions
      we wrestle with. The only
      answer is gleaning how art can

      move so slowly through time
      as if all its incarnations would
      combust if they were to meet.

Portrait of a life

(after Félix González-Torres)

I believe the seasons of love   will give us our direction   even as
they decay   one after the other and we slip   from our foundations.
I have no name for it   but I know it like the gasp   in my right knee
after a run.   I want to prove many small things   simultaneously

in order to establish a life   making sense of our methods of assemblage:
borders and corners first or bursts of similar colours?   I take from the past
as a way to bind myself   to everything that ultimately   disappears.
My family as a wall of Mahjong tiles.   My lovers as candy wrappers

strewn through coat pockets. My friends moving across seas   to follow
their own lights.   We fall for instant satisfaction because that's what makes
the bitterness of daily life bearable   but we forget it's the everlasting that is
the sweetener we should be chasing. I used to think I'd get lost in the wide-

screen view of the world like a small town rubbed away   into the crease of
every map. I made friends with this unease. As a child I swallowed chicken
bones thinking this would build a fortress   around my heart. What will
protect me from my own thoughts? I make grand gestures to leave behind

more than just a few lines in the death notices. There's something at the end
of every road, even if you can't see it with the naked eye: it's knowing that
one man's fortune is another man's motivational poster. As much as I'd like
to build something permanent I know I have only so much I can give away.

Spoiler alerts for the end of the world

Every year is a year of life and death, regardless of which animals are nesting in your rainy-day accounts with unsolicited advice. The year of alarm is how you'll refer to the evergreen memory of police forming barricades at a peaceful protest while teenagers extinguish teargas with road cones and water bottles. We fail ourselves, time and time again, without pausing to consider whether our failures can be undone. The best way to kill a snake is to sever its head from its body. The best way to save the future is to sever the present from its tracks. In a way leaning into the smoke of our burning world is good practice for how we'll choke on everything else we love that's slowly killing us. The sky is telling us the red flush we gather to cheer on isn't celebration—it's our outlook being bought by the highest bidder who will dedicate an entire chapter about this betrayal in his best-selling memoir, a fixture of every Whitcoulls Top 100 Books list for the foreseeable future. I've eaten my own heart only to find I'm allergic to melodrama and yet I'd do it all again just for the exposure. I've cut my own brakes just to give the other doomed ones a sporting chance. There have been so many red flags hoisted around us broadcasting spoilers from their poles. I know I'll only ever see so much blue sky in my lifetime, but what good is having strength to change the world when all I'll have to show for it is a certificate of participation? What I'd give for God to emerge from their celestial spa bath, point at me in my dressing gown and scream, 'WE HAVE A WINNER!!' Instead, everybody gets a turn on the spinning wheel of despair until it's clear we've outlasted the stars' attention span, and the ruins of our past, present and future will coalesce as one glittering monument—a place for us to leave unfinished copies of self-help books we bought in our most open-minded states before the sirens, before the ladders we walked under collapsed. How to live, how to die, how anyone makes it through a day without punching themselves in the face is the greatest mystery.

Super model minority—Reincarnations

I was a sky   when a sky meant untapped potential.

Now a sky   is the end of days—the unpredictable

nature of a world   melting and freezing at the same time.

I was a river   when a river meant speeding ahead

into the space   between new and remembered—always

a perilous chase.   Now a river is the earth turning against itself

in slow motion   a sick vein carrying needles to the brain.

I was a line   when a line was something you memorised.

Now a line   is what I bolt from with my flaming sword and shield

running blind   into a resolution that's been decided

for me. I had   an idea that would separate the heroes

from the thieves   but throwing my body against their walls

has taught me   a flag can't contain everything, but it says enough that

they raise their gun   whenever they see me approaching

Photogenesis

out of dusk light and straight into shepherds' blood

    smeared across the sky—I stand under the future

and wonder who will guide me to rest when I'm all

    but gone—whether the future is finite or infinite

is something I'll never know—at worst there will be no

    reasons to pop champagne—no delight in apocalypse

when we're made of flammable histories—fire won't

    slow down—it knows nothing about consideration

or when to call it quits—its speed is the rate of hope

    conceding—of disarmament breaking into our

homes while we sleep—but if we were glowing lights under

    crushing waves of smoke and ash—if our biology

were designed to signal restlessness and desperation by matching

    heat with heat—tell me who would be the brightest—

and how many lives would I have to surrender

to reach into the sound of my body tearing itself

apart asking for help—to retrieve a dream that doesn't end

with darkness being crowned the victor—some

of us kneel at altars—some of us offer the dead everything

they'll need when they leave us—I remember scraps of

my past (what if that is all I'll have to take with me?)—I

wander the present as a thief of what's gone before—

stealing promises from one lover to gift to the next and expecting

the same response—that's the corner I've backed

myself into—to have no recollection of how I got there and

what to do next while my eyes are alight and

my skin gives away my secrets—even with the presence of light

we're no wiser than we were before we trusted

the sky to not combust or the earth to stay in one place—I still

think light is proof that something is happening

right before us—even when my vision stutters and I have no

reason to believe in hope—even when the deceits and

machinations of the present day seem unavoidable—it's

enough to look up at a sky blushing red and

see possibility—to not worry how the end will reveal itself

Funeral arrangements for the end of the world

All the clocks have been stopped and all the cell towers have crumbled, their harsh greys taken by the slow greens of dystopian vines and weeds. To say goodbye is to give yourself a chance to wake up, but how do you bury an entire world? The answer lies in the loss of your senses and the gift of hindsight. First, you must pronounce the world ended by recognising all of its successes and failures. Then you'll be directed to a path to walk on into the endless next. Having said that, don't be mistaken: this poem isn't a list of demands or instructions. It's a bouquet of yellow chrysanthemums pressed between the pages of an almanac. It's snapping your fingers at a poetry slam like you're in the rumble to end all rumbles. It's an In Memoriam montage of Indigenous place names. You can lift ritual from any other ending—rinse, repeat—as so many other deaths and extinctions have been marked. The year of apple and snake was an ending, as were the years of plague, war and love lost. The pattern is whatever you choose to see. We have worried ourselves sick over not knowing what comes after The End. This poem doesn't have the answers, but if you want to hear that it's resurrection, I will tell you: after The End comes resurrection. If you want the comfort of being remembered, I will tell you: after The End is the memory of your being passed down the line like an heirloom. I can tell you heaven is a ring, or confirm the existence of an undiscovered nothingness. I can tell you when it's safe to open your eyes. Regardless of what you want to believe in, you must be prepared. Now this poem becomes a list of instructions. When you arrive at the gate between fields, exchange the jade cicada in your mouth for the next rotation. I imagine the options will be limited to begin with—weightless names and skins so bland you won't be noticed at first. Pass through the gate and walk until you reach a door. Knock, and hope that whatever's behind it is kind.

Notes and acknowledgements

The Chen Chen quote that introduces 'Wish list—Permadeath' is taken from his essay 'I'm Not Here to Play the Suffering Minority for White Readers', published on Electric Literature (14 June 2018).

'Stability (Version)' is based on the poem 'Stability', which first appeared in *AUP New Poets 4* (2011). That poem was written about my maternal great-grandfather.

The poem by the Canadian poet Chris Tse referred to in '謝—I'm sorry I'm a Chris Tse' is 'I'm Sorry I'm a Christian'.

'The Magician—Notes on distraction' was written for, and first performed at, the gala night of the 2019 Dunedin Writers and Readers Festival. The featured writers were asked to write and share a piece based on the theme of 'distraction'.

The poems in part two are based on the colours of the LGBT pride flag designed by Gilbert Baker. The original flag featured eight colours; the more common contemporary version features just six. Each of the poems in this sequence takes its inspiration from the meanings attributed to the eight colours of the original flag.

'Poetry to make boys cry' references the song 'I Didn't Just Come Here to Dance' performed by Carly Rae Jepsen, from her album *Emotion* (2015).

The lyrics quoted in 'The other side of the glass' are taken from the song 'Flawless (Go to the City)' performed by George Michael, from his album *Patience* (2004).

'What's fun until it gets weird?' takes its title from a card in the game Cards Against Humanity.

'White flag' takes its title from the Grant Lingard artwork of the same name. The artwork is a flag stitched together from white Jockey Y-fronts.

'BOY OH BOY OH BOY OH BOY' was inspired by the art and poetry of Sam Duckor-Jones.

'Geometric Growth' takes its title from the Guy Ngan sculpture of the same name. The sculpture was originally installed in 1979 at the corner of Victoria and Mercer streets in Wellington. It was removed in 1989 to make way for the development of Civic Square and kept in storage. In 2006, it was reinstalled in its current location on Wakefield Street next to the Michael Fowler Centre carpark.

'Portrait of a life' was inspired by Félix González-Torres' series of participatory artworks. One such artwork, 'Untitled (Portrait of Ross in L. A.)' is an allegorical portrait of González-Torres' late lover Ross Laycock, who passed away from AIDS-related complications. The artwork is a pile of candy weighing 175 pounds (Laycock's body weight when healthy). Viewers are invited to take candy from the work.

Many thanks to the editors and publishers of the following publications in which some of these poems first appeared: *Aotearotica*, *ART Paper*, *bath magg*, *Best New Zealand Poems*, *Landfall*, New Zealand Poetry Shelf, *Our Selves*, *Queen Mob's Teahouse: Teh Book*, The Satellites Lockdown Calendar, *The Spinoff*, *Sport*, *Stasis*, *Turbine | Kapohau*, *VERB Journal* and *Wasafiri*.

My heartfelt thanks to Creative New Zealand, for a grant that enabled me to complete the first draft of this book—Auckland University Press (Katharina Bauer, Sophia Broom, Lauren Donald and Sam Elworthy)—Emma Neale—Greg Simpson—Madison Hamill—Rose Lu—Nina Mingya Powles—Helen Rickerby—Francis Cooke, Louise Wallace and Gem Wilder—Emma Barnes—Paula Green—Emily Writes—Claire Mabey and Andrew Laking—Rosabel Tan—Show Ponies—Nathan Joe, Jane Yonge and the cast and crew of *Scenes from a Yellow Peril*.

Huge love to my parents, Jimmy and Kathy—Leight, Jo and Maddie—Michael—my family and friends—the extended Gibson whānau—the Taupō crew.

Chris Tse was born and raised in Lower Hutt. He studied English literature and film at Victoria University of Wellington, where he also completed an MA in creative writing at the International Institute of Modern Letters. Tse was one of three poets featured in *AUP New Poets 4* (2011), and his work has appeared in publications in New Zealand and overseas. His first collection *How to be Dead in a Year of Snakes* (2014) won the Jessie Mackay Award for Best First Book of Poetry, and his second book *HE'S SO MASC* was published to critical acclaim in 2018. He is co-editor of AUP's *Out Here: An Anthology of Takatāpui and LGBTQIA+ Writers from Aotearoa*, published in 2021.